Sketch Book With Framed Pages

150 PAGES ~ DRAWING ~ SKETCHING

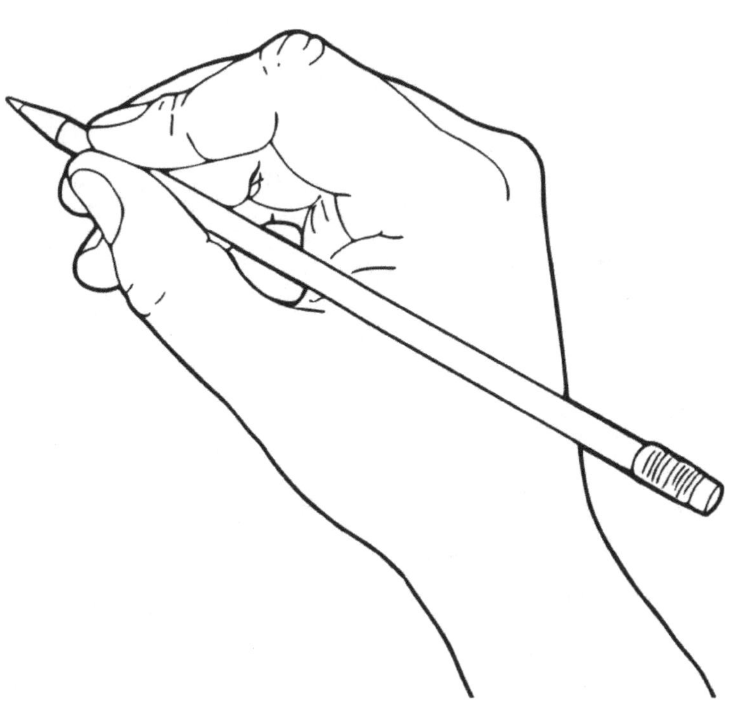

www.ingramcontent.com/pod-product-compliance
Lightning Source LLC
Chambersburg PA
CBHW081000170526
45158CB00010B/2853
9781073125586